COSMETIC TATTOOING

BUSINESS SET UP AND MARKETING ESSENTIALS

LEILA MOORE

Copyright © 2017 by Leila Moore. All Rights Reserved.

No part of this publication may be reproduced, distributed, or transmitted in any form or by any means, including photocopying, recording, or other electronic or mechanical methods, or by any information storage and retrieval system without the prior written permission of the author, except in the case of very brief quotations embodied in critical reviews and certain other noncommercial uses permitted by copyright law.

Table of Contents

Why I Wrote this Book... 4

Introduction... 6

Starting Out as a Cosmetic Tattooist....................... 8

Setting Up Your Website.. 12

Going That One Bit Extra... 19

Getting That First Client.. 22

A Word on Promo Deals... 31

Referrals and Networking... 33

Why Traditional Advertising is Changing............ 36

    Google and Other Search Providers................... 36

    Facebook... 42

    Instagram 47

    Twitter.. 61

Reviews... 67

Leverage Yourself.. 70

Mistakes to avoid... 72

Conclusion 78

One Last Thing… 79

Why I Wrote this Book

As a self-confessed "computer noob" with an introverted personality to match, I found it quite hard to openly market myself as a new cosmetic tattooist. Whilst my permanent make-up (PMU) training gave me the confidence to undertake new clients, I found that I lacked the business mindset to build my brand. I knew I could do good work, the problem was, no one else knew! This book is a combination of the marketing strategies which I learned from scratch. Hours of Google searching, researching techniques, and trial and error of best practice methods have all been compiled into this book. I wish I'd had someone to talk me through all the intricacies of marketing early on. It would have saved many a night where I questioned the feasibility of my business success, let alone all that emotional eating…

The permanent make-up industry is a highly exciting and lucrative field when done right. This guide aims to facilitate new and existing artists in building their brands so they can focus on core business - giving clients great service. It is by no means a wholly comprehensive manual, but it enables practitioners to learn some strategies which have helped me and many peers to fill client bookings. Dedicating a few hours a week to marketing is essential for the longevity of your business. I hope you enjoy the read and find a strategy which really helps your business to stand out amongst competitors!

Leila

Introduction

The cosmetic tattooing industry has experienced a huge uplift in client interest over the past few years. With the advent of feather eyebrow and ombré powder techniques, as well as the return of the thicker brow trend, permanent make-up artists are reaping the rewards of this newfound popularity.

Many have undertaken PMU training to capitalize on the lucrative tattooing industry. The upfront investment in this form of education can be quite pricey and easily exceed tens of thousands in business set up costs. Unfortunately, having a diploma within this field does not go hand in hand with operating a successful tattooing enterprise.

Cosmetic tattooists often have a beauty therapy or esthetician background. Regardless of how skillful their technique may be, this does not guarantee that they will have full bookings or an influx of keen clientele. They are not trained in the fundamentals of marketing, competitive analysis, or progressive advertising. The old school pamphlet drop-offs no longer cut it in this industry. To operate in today's modern world requires an understanding of savvy marketing and the dominance of social media. These skills are rarely taught within the PMU space and can leave some vulnerable to business failure, despite best efforts.

This book will guide you through the key aspects to promote your cosmetic tattooing services. The methods outlined here will enable you to differentiate yourself from others and build strategic advantage above your competitors. Although good, quality, PMU work will speak for itself and generate client leads, it will not serve you to be complacent in this moving market. Ensuring that your name is top of mind when people consider getting a cosmetic tattoo should be an essential business goal.

Starting Out as a Cosmetic Tattooist

You have just finished your course, obtained the appropriate licenses and insurance, now what? If you already have a presence in the beauty industry, then you would probably add cosmetic tattooing to your service menu. Alternatively, you may be someone who has started anew and need to build this exciting career from scratch. In this case, there are some critical decisions which need to be made early on:

- Will you operate under the salon name, your own name (i.e. Amy Claren Cosmetic Tattooing), or a more generic name such as Permanent Beauty Inc.? This has implications as you may spend time investing in brand building only to discover that you want to expand in the future, or want to sell your business but it is not viable...unless you happen to find another Amy Claren. Ensure that the name you pick is available to use as a registered business, website domain address, and across social media channels for consistency.

- Are you setting up in a market where there is a lot of competition? How will you stand out from the rest? Do an online search of the cosmetic tattooists in your area and compare aspects such as pricing, experience, and overall professionalism of their branding. Various options to consider include offering a cheaper service than others, creating a more premium brand at a higher price point, or adding touch up services for free instead of charging etc... Note that with PMU, it is often a case of "you get what you pay for" and many clients are willing to fork out that extra cash to insure against a poor outcome. Consumers are more forgiving with services such as haircuts and manicures so don't sell yourself short too early.

- What quality of materials will you use? In terms of pigment line, needle brand, type of tattooing machine and so forth, there can be a huge disparity in costs. Some artists opt to buy the cheapest of everything to keep overheads down. This approach is understandably tempting as you have already spent so much on training and set up. It is also quite painful to compare the price of items imported from China and eBay to more reputable industry suppliers. However, the risk of poor client outcomes is high in this instance. You may experience a range of problems (which are not immediately obvious) such as unsterilized or bent needles, pigment color changes in clients, and numbing creams just not doing their job. Try to compromise instead by buying cheaper disposables which do not directly impact treatments (one-use aprons, Q tips, rulers and cleansing wipes from your supermarket). Invest in the best items you can afford when it comes to actual tattooing tools.

- Where will you practice from? Depending on the regulations of your locale, there may be the option to work from a rented salon room, a home based set up, or even on a mobile basis (this is not recommended as it is difficult to control for hygiene and cross contamination). Think of the benefits of each and compare pricing. If you lease a room from a salon, there may be the added advantage of client referrals who have come for other services. The overheads are usually lower if you arrange a commission split or day rate too. Once you have a more established brand, it may be more practical to set up your own studio.

Setting Up Your Website

As well as sorting out your branding and logo, this will need to align with a strong web presence or site. Some cosmetic tattooists operate successfully without a website and rely solely on a Facebook business page. This approach is something you can consider, however, it puts you at risk of opportunity loss. Having your own site will allow locals to find you on directories and present your brand as highly professional. You can also provide information on a "Frequently Asked Questions" page to avoid responding to the same kind of email queries. This time saving can be invaluable when you are operating a business and need to direct focus away from admin.

Setting up a website does not have to cost you an arm and a leg either. Fully functional sites can be developed and hosted for as little as $200. You just need to be tactful with hiring professionals to do the job. Of course, it is up to you if you prefer to invest in hiring a boutique firm to assist you through the steps. Here is a high level summary of steps you need to take if you prefer the DIY approach:

- All websites need to be hosted. This means that you need to purchase a hosting plan from a business that provides the technologies needed for the webpage to be viewed on the Internet. Popular and affordable choices include GoDaddy or HostGator.

- Secure a domain name. You can also purchase these from the latter providers and check if your preferred combination is available. Note that careful thought should be put into this – you may want to check if there are PMU businesses with similar names and update yours accordingly to avoid confusion. Nobody wants to be served with a legal battle over naming rights.

- Browse online for site ideas which you would like to replicate or use as inspiration for your own business. There are also a number of custom design themes which can be purchased from web developers.

- Get a business logo. Use this design on all your marketing materials and uploaded on your site. Once you have chosen a website and brand theme, commission a graphics designer to create a logo. This can be done quite inexpensively on sites such as Fiverr.com at a high quality.

- Depending on your level of IT skills or ability, you can choose to outsource the remaining work. Use a site such as Upwork.com or Freelancer.com to post a task detailing what you would like done. Make sure that you are clear on the terms and expected pricing. Web developers based from other countries where the wage differential is significant, generally India or Philippines, will bid on your post for the opportunity to undertake the work. Read through their feedback from other hires and make an informed choice. Although there may be some grammatical errors or slight language barrier (you can control for this by providing all the content anyway), the quality of work delivered is usually top notch, and for only a fraction of the price of onshore services!

In detailing your brief for a business website, there are a number of features you should request. These elements include:

About Me/About Our Business
This doesn't have to be comprehensive. Clients just like to know that the person who will be permanently tattooing their face is qualified to do so. You don't have to mention that you only got your accreditation the week prior...

Email Submission Form
Instead of just providing a contact email or

phone number for clients to use, request an in-built email submission form to be made on your site. This makes it much easier for people to type out a query and submit it directly to you from the site (as opposed to copying your email address then logging into their own accounts to send something through). Always try to reduce the steps a potential customer needs to make to engage with your business.

Online Booking Portal

This is not an essential feature but if you do get inundated with clients, it is certainly helpful to reduce admin. As studies show that 35% of appointments are made during non-business hours, adding online booking can have a dramatic impact. Many programs can be used to do this for a small subscription fee. You will need to input your free slots and clients can nominate and hold a time for a percentage deposit on their credit card. This will also deter people from last minute cancellations (a big problem in the PMU industry!). Make sure you outline your booking terms and timeframe for refunds or appointment changes.

Social Media Buttons

This allows for ease of access to your Facebook, Instagram, and Twitter pages where your work portfolio should be regularly updated. More followers equals more exposure!

Portfolio or Client Photos

Ensure that all displayed work has prior agreement from your client for public display. There are also apps which allow your Instagram or Facebook posts to automatically be updated onto your website. This will save in duplication of work and ensure you have the same presence on all forums. Do not be tempted to post work that is not your own, this often occurs with new artists and it is highly unethical. Those who do this are likely to experience repercussions when the client is disappointed with the poorer quality results. Practice over time really does make a huge difference to your work as well as confidence.

Service List with Prices

This is pretty self explanatory. Customers appreciate transparency and will trust that no surprise extras are added. You will find that "how much for......??" will be one of your most commonly received questions from prospective clients, regardless of whether it is detailed on your site or not. At least having them listed means that you can just flick them a link each time.

Location Map and Opening Hours

Again, this is a no-brainer. Having a map will help with clients who are looking for a PMU artist near home, or to minimize the risk of late arrivals to appointments. Google maps is able to be integrated into your website for a live version. If you are located in a busy area, suggest some parking areas (with a minimum 2 to 3 hour duration) to help out your clients.

Going That One Bit Extra....

Although not essential, if you really want to differentiate yourself or if there are many competing sites, consider the following:

Photo/s of Yourself

It is human nature that many of us base our judgment on appearances. As cosmetic tattooing is an industry which relies on confidence and trust in your practitioner, some PMU artists opt to have professional photos taken for their site. This is usually used in the "About Me" or "Meet Your Artist" page. Some opt to use photos where they are in the process of a treatment. Think about what will best reflect your branding and whether this kind of snapshot will add credibility.

Client Testimonials

Feedback from satisfied and happy clients can be an effective and subtle way of making a sales pitch. They show potential customers that you are trustworthy, skilled, and an expert in the field. Note that a fake review is often quite obvious – your website visitors can see through this and it shows a lack of integrity. Matching a testimonial to a before/after photo can add credibility to the endorsement. If you don't have any testimonials, simply email your customers or models and ask them to provide some feedback if they are happy to do so.

Videos

If a picture is worth a thousand words, a video could very well be worth a thousand sales. Video marketing is a very underrated trick used by savvy entrepreneurs. This form of advertising has been found to significantly increase visitor engagement and conversion into paying clients. Studies show that clients who view websites which use video are anywhere from 64 to 85% more likely to buy. In fact, including a video link in your newsletter or email listing can increase click through's to your site or offer by 200%. Consider what kind of video is appropriate for your business. Perhaps it is a reel of you talking about the types of tattooing methods and what customers should look for in a PMU artist (without directly saying pick me!). In any case, ensure that it is professionally done and edited. A poorly made video can have a counterproductive impact and put off prospective clients.

Email Subscriber Pop-Up or Sign Up Tab
Many clients visit your site but hesitate to follow through with booking an appointment. They may still be making a decision with treatments or seeing if you are currently offering any promos. Use a subscriber tab to collect visitor details as a warm-lead and send out regular email promotions or newsletters. Consumers are conditioned to trust someone they have more familiarity with. You'd be surprised at how many additional bookings that this technique can generate.

Getting That First Client

Taking on your first client who is not a model or whilst under the supervision of your trainer can be incredibly daunting. Permanently marking one's face is a big responsibility and should be done only if you feel capable. Once you are appropriately licensed and set up to practice, it may take a while to gain traction and finally generate income.

Many prospective customers are interested in how much experience you have and may request a review of your portfolio. Whether or not you have a portfolio at this point depends largely on the training you undertook, and how many practical assessments on real models you did. Other options are for you to leverage your network of brave friends and family to work on. They tend to be more patient and allow you to take your time with treatments.

If this is not an option, another approach is to post an advertisement up on forums such as

Craigslist asking for cosmetic tattooing models. You can offer this service for free or for a subsidized amount compared to your usual pricing. Be transparent with respondents about your experience if asked and commence if they are comfortable to do so. A sample advertisement is provided below, note that it has been worded so that the offer is framed as an opportunity that models will have to apply for. People tend to respond well to exclusivity and you are able to tailor the ad to your liking.

COSMETIC TATTOO PORTFOLIO MODELS REQUIRED $200

An opportunity to have your eyebrows tattooed using the feathering technique by a fully qualified and insured technician. We charge $650 for our feather brows, however, many clients prefer to keep their photos private.

In order to build our portfolio, we are offering this service for $200 (initial appointment only - touch up is $145 if required) for a limited number of individuals. You must have no previous tattooing or correction work for coverage.

The service will include:

- A full consultation included in the 2-3 hour appointment
- Colour selection for skin tone
- Eyebrow design which suits your facial structure
- Use of only high quality and industry leading pigments, needles and techniques

If you are interested, please send an email a picture of your bare brow photo to xxxxx@gmail.com. Those approved as models are required to give consent for before/after shots (we only display pictures of your eyes and eyebrows and not of full face).

This is a genuine offer and we hope this will be a great arrangement for both parties.

You can also leverage your local networks to source some clientele. Undertake a Google search of the beauty salons which you feel would be a good fit to partner with. Ensure that they do not currently offer cosmetic tattooing, and establish if they seem to be a popular choice for clients (e.g. via Facebook Page likes, Instagram followers, Yelp Reviews). Compile this information in a listing or spreadsheet as shown below:

Salons to Approach	Existing PMU Service?	Location	Owner or Manager	Popularity	Email & Phone
Revive Skin	No	San Antonio	Mya Brent	511 Facebook Likes 2300 Instagram Followers 75 Yelp Reviews	info@revive.com (210) 301-0307
Bella Spa Salon	No	San Antonio	Lydia Stott	1230 Facebook Likes 4100 Instagram Followers 110 Yelp Reviews	info@bella.com (210) 256-5100

Once you have identified which salons you would like to target, give the manager a call to introduce yourself and ask to email through a service offering such as this:

[INSERT BUSINESS LOGO]

To the Salon Owner,

I am a fully qualified, insured and licensed permanent makeup artist trained under strict American standards. I love providing high quality outcomes to all clients with results that are natural and complementary to facial structure, skin tone and hair color. My clients are often delighted with their results and how their natural beauty has been enhanced by cosmetic tattooing.

With a mindset of continuous improvement, I keep up to date with new techniques and continue to attend advanced workshops and training to hone my skills. Driven by a desire to provide the best customer service and permanent makeup experience, I focus exclusively on cosmetic tattooing, performing all procedures using only the industry's leading pigments and equipment.

I currently operate under my business "Amy Claren Cosmetic Tattooing" and source my own clientele. I am at the stage of expansion and am interested in working with your salon in a collaborative arrangement. For example, as the salon you would book clients in for a specific day and in return receive a percentage of the service fee for each treatment. Recent beauty trends show that adding cosmetic tattooing to your service menu is a great way to boost business. The feather eyebrow or hairstroke simulation technique is particularly popular and is my key service offering.

I have provided a summary of details below for further reference. Please free to contact me to discuss this opportunity further.

Many thanks,

Amy

Service Offering

- Provide cosmetic tattooing to clients on behalf of your salon on an at-call basis. I am quite flexible, reliable, and can work a wide range of hours. Happy to commit to a trial period for you to assess service demand and quality of my work

- Supply all of the equipment necessary to undertake the treatments (e.g. anesthesia, pigments, digital machinery, medical grade consumables etc.)
- Provide legally compliant documentation and client forms for cosmetic tattooing which can be updated to reflect your branding
- Cross promote your brand on my social network (Facebook 535 Likes/Instagram 850 followers)

Sample Profit Analysis

- You can view my pricing structure here: www.amyclaren.com/pricing
- Hypothetically, each treatment takes 2 hours at a rate of $600. On any given day I can take on up to 4 clients (4 x $600 total treatment cost = $2400). My offering to your salon is for a 20% commission in return for room usage and client referral = $480 daily your share
- I charge very reasonable market rates given my use of high quality materials. Feather brow tattooing can command up to $1000 and is

quite viral in popularity when promoted properly
- Training current staff internally to perform cosmetic tattooing would cost upwards of 10k before you see a return on investment
- I am also open to providing initial tattooing services on promotion (e.g. rates discounted or referral bonus)

Requirements
- You must be registered by your local health authority salon laws (generally this is something you will already have as an operating salon)
- A clean room with the following:
    - Hand basin fitted with hot and cold water
    - Treatment bed and stool/chair
    - Stand or table to place tools on
    - Appropriate waste disposal standards

You can change the text as per your own business practices, but ensure that the focus is on the **benefit to the salon!** Managers are often spammed with promotional material or are targeted by skincare brands to partner with. Stand out and sell yourself by offering a win-win scenario. If they are interested in your sales spiel, then you could further leverage the relationship. Ask to be featured on their newsletter/mailing list or use their Facebook page to promote the new service offered. Using this approach, you could quickly target hundreds or even thousands of prospective clients within your area!

A Word on Promo Deals

One option that may cross your mind when starting out is to use sites such as Groupon or Slickdeals. Admittedly, this is one way to quickly get your brand out there in leveraging their huge online followings. On the surface, it sounds like a great way to market your business until you look at the figures. The usual discounting rate is 50% off of normal service fees, with the site taking another 50% cut of commission on every sale. You will effectively be left with a 25% margin after everything, and this can be completely eaten up by salon overheads or materials used.

Moreover, you run the risk of damaging your brand as consumers may rate it as a second tier service. You don't want to become the artist who is known for discounting or where you can grab a bargain. Logic would lead some to presume that resorting to a deals site means that your work isn't high in demand. Clients know that in the PMU industry, there is often a waiting period to secure appointments with popular tattooists.

This is a field in which people will invest in quality. Note that if you do opt to use a deal to promote your new business, the webpage will still be found on Google long-after, albeit with the discount archived. Prospective clients are likely to know that you previously reduced fees and may be put off or request a price match from you. Ensure that you value your brand, otherwise you will get the wrong kind of reputation.

Referrals and Networking

Your network is a powerful tool in sourcing out new business. Friends, family and colleagues are often more than happy to support and lend a hand if you reach out. You would be surprised at the amount of people who would like to get their eyebrows or liner done, and prefer to have someone they know and trust to do it.

Forming Partnerships

Who else in the business world works with your target client group? Go one further and incentivize people for recommending you. Speak to friends or acquaintances who are in the beauty industry and who regularly engage with prospective clients. Some tattooists collaborate with make-up artists and refer the other to share client pools. You could also offer them a cut of the tattooing fee, say $50, per person they send over. Make a visit to skin clinics and cosmetic surgeons in the area and ask to leave your brochures there. The subset of people who visit those types of establishments are often more open to getting a cosmetic tattoo, compared to the general public. If any of your clients mention that they were referred from a particular clinic, then reimburse the clinic for the gesture. Over time it may end up being a very lucrative arrangement for both parties.

If you are quite engaged in the PMU community (online forums, attending training courses etc.), then you are likely to have colleagues or friends who are also in the industry. Often these artists are located in different states and have a large client base if they are particularly talented. They will on occasion be asked if they can recommend another cosmetic tattooist who is closer to home, as many people are unable to travel very far for their treatment. This is your opportunity to step up and make this a reciprocal arrangement. Engage with fellow cosmetic tattooists who aren't in direct competition with you and send remotely located clients to them.

You will also find that existing clients are the best free advertising you could ask for. When someone is happy with the job you have done they are likely to share it with their network. It is very common for entire friendship groups to be treated by the one cosmetic tattooist. If you are still growing your portfolio then it may be worth offering a "bring a friend" promo for a discounted rate.

Why Traditional Advertising is Changing

The growth of social media and online forums has created a huge shift in conventional marketing. In this modern age, people are quick to consume new information and share it on their smartphones to their networks. A business operator who relies solely on brochure drop-offs and local newspaper advertisements is likely to see low uptake. Although print adverts are still viable in some industries, the vast majority are moving to more innovative ways of sourcing business. Traditional advertising has been superseded by online methods. This allows brands to engage with customers and foster a relationship of trust over time. The following are essential tools, and the ways in which you can utilize them, for business success:

Google and Other Search Providers

Do you know where your salon website currently ranks in Google? If someone searches online for "best feather eyebrow tattoo Texas", will your business even show up in search results? And if it does, how many pages down in rankings does it appear? Studies have shown that 33% of prospective customers click on the first result shown by Google. Just 17% visit the second result. And the traffic only reduces from there. Ensure that you are not invisible to new clients by being one step ahead.

Search Engine Optimization (SEO), is how businesses get their websites to appear in results when prospects search for services in their geographic area. From a marketing perspective, working on your SEO can be the most cost effective way to drive qualified, ongoing traffic to your website. Unless you are exceptionally tech-savvy, this is a task which will need to be outsourced to a credible company. Be vary of the many offshore, cheaper service offerings who employ black hat tactics to get your site to rank. You may find yourself penalized by search engines over the long term for taking this short cut. To give you an idea of changes which can be made (some undertaken by yourself and some outsourced), some key SEO strategies include:

- Ensuring that your website looks good on mobile devices. Nowadays everyone owns a smartphone or tablet with which they use to surf the web daily. Laptops or desktop computers have been superseded for the convenience of on-the-go information. Research has shown that up to 60% of online visitors will view your website from a smartphone or tablet. If it is incompatible or hard to navigate, then visitors will quickly leave your page to search for a different website. This is a huge potential loss of income. Google will also determine your search result ranking based on how mobile-friendly your site is.

- Register your business details, contact number, and website on Google and other credible search providers. You can then "claim" the business pages as your own and respond to any reviews in a professional manner. Some sites allow you to input this once and will on-forward the registration details to all other providers on your behalf. Be picky with the forums that you submit your details with as you may find yourself spammed with marketing calls or emails.

- Write a blog or article. This will ideally relate to PMU and new developments in cosmetic tattooing. Website visitors particularly like the bullet point type articles such as "10 Things to Look for in a Cosmetic Tattooist" or "5 Ways to Increase Retention of Your Tattoo". As well as being a fun exercise to do, customers will also regard you as an expert in this field. By using certain keywords in your blog section which enables you to be found online, your ranking on Google will increase significantly!

- Approaching keywords strategically. These are words and phrases that people type into a search engine to find websites that match what they are looking for. Some keywords get hundreds of thousands of unique searches a day while others get a couple of hundred. For example, there might be 1500 monthly searches for "eyebrow tattoo Texas" which makes it highly competitive. A look at other potential keywords terms may show that 400 people search for "microblading artist Texas". Fewer PMU business sites may be competing to rank for this term so you may amend your target keywords accordingly. Capturing the eye of 400 hits monthly is better than ranking on the fifth Google page for 1500 searches and never being found!

- From a more technical perspective, improving your search rankings can also include the optimization of on-site elements across your site. Using quality tagged images, increasing your site's load speed, and adjusting navigation and internal links are amongst some of the key tactics used.

SEO is a multi-faceted approach to driving your online presence. Whilst it can be complicated and highly technical, getting it right can be the factor that leads you to huge success.

Facebook

Facebook is an essential tool for cosmetic tattooists. Nearly all consumers use the internet to search for local businesses, and most of them are on Facebook. This site is the biggest social networking platform in the world, with more than a billion active users. Through your personal account, you can create a business page on Facebook (people won't be able to link to your own profile unless you make it obvious). This page is a lot like a regular Facebook profile but for brands and businesses. Use this as a forum to interact with potential clients and to provide live updates of promotions and photos of your work.

This type of profile also allows you to use Facebook's page insights tool. The tool, accessible from your Facebook page's admin menu, provides valuable information on follower activity. For example, it can tell you what time most people view your content so you can plan your promotions. It can also tell you which type of posts are most popular and liked by your audience.

Make sure that this page truly reflects your brand. Use your business logo as the primary photo for your page, and pick a cover photo that is attractive and showcases your best work. Type up a brief bio to describe your brand, and choose a web address which corresponds closely to your business name. Facebook Page URLs appear in the form of www.facebook.com/(yourbrand).

Once you have done the initial set-up, create opportunities for your followers to interact with your page by adding engaging content, creating competitions, and replying to any questions. Personal interaction with customers fosters trust in your brand and encourages more people to view your page. Here are some tips and ideas to consider when using Facebook for your business:

Be Consistent

Ensure that you are consistent with posting on your page, if you don't post frequently enough people will lose interest and unfollow or unlike. Post too often and you'll risk annoying them away. Use the insights tool to create a posting schedule specific to your product and audience. There is no point in showing off your latest work when everyone is asleep and not looking at their feed. Consider both frequency and time of day. Studies have shown that 5 to 10 posts a week is the ideal amount for most businesses.

In the PMU industry, you can't just pause a client treatment mid way to post on Facebook just because analyses have shown that 1pm is your optimum time. There are various apps and programs out there (such as Buffer or Postcron) that will create a schedule for your posts and publish them at the best time of the day based on your followers' activity.

What's Your Message?

Think about what posts you want to share on your page. Facebook is all about authenticity, so if a business does not focus on customers in a way that feels genuine, prospective clients will see right through it. Quotes, memes, before and after shots, behind the scenes photos, introduction of new products or services, or even video posts can go viral. The most successful Facebook posts that drive people to comment, share and like are visual so utilize this rather than just a text-based announcement for your promos.

Pay For Exposure

Consider advertising on Facebook if you want to reach specific groups or followers of your page. Facebook allows you to target ads based on everything from demographics and location to purchasing behavior and interests. As a PMU artist, your sample targeted group may be those in your specific area, between the ages of 22 to

45, who previously liked pages related to eyebrow or make-up tips.

Run Calendar Specials

Think about opportunities to promote your services which coincide with special dates. Mother's Day, Valentines, Easter, Halloween etc. can all be leveraged to offer unique discounts or promotions. Clients love a good deal and even if they aren't keen on getting a cosmetic tattoo, they may share your post or tag friends who might be interested. This all results in a larger follower base and has a cumulative effect in building brand awareness over time.

Instagram

If you had to leverage only one tool for marketing your business, then this is your holy grail. This photo sharing app has single handedly launched successful careers for many cosmetic tattooists. Whilst you still need to be talented at what you do, it certainly helps to have a forum like Instagram to promote your work. A study by Forrester (2016) found that the app delivered 25% more brand engagement over other social platforms, whilst the average converted sale was $67. This is because people on average retain 80% of visual information as opposed to other forms of advertising which are read or listened to.

This section is not a basic Instagram guide on how to use buttons or upload photos. You can find plenty of free guides online for that. This is for people who already understand how to use Instagram's features but want a more in depth knowledge of tested marketing strategies. The following are essential steps in building your profile:

Set Up Your Profile

Use your business name or a close variation if possible. Upload your logo design as a profile picture. Using the 150 character allowance, write up a brief bio of what you do, add your website link (arrow or finger emoji's pointing to your website address help to drive conversions as they work as a take-action cue), and contact details. You can also configure your account so that it is linked to your Facebook business page – any photos you put up will be concurrently posted. Don't make the critical mistake of leaving your settings on private so prospective followers can not see your uploads.

Do Your Research

Instagram allows you to use a maximum of 30 hashtags per post. In short, tagged posts enable people to tap the hashtag to view a page that shows all photos and videos that have been uploaded which match that word. So a potential client could search the term "eyebrowtattoo" and your post which is tagged with that word will appear in the feed.

Utilize this functionality to build a following and get your brand out there. To work out which popular hashtags you should use to be easily found, use free programs such as Iconosquare and Webstagram. They will help you to review trending words in the cosmetic tattooing niche to form a list. Some common ones are "eyebrowfeathering", "browsonfleek", "cosmetictattoo", and "microblading". View the profiles of popular PMU artists and copy the hashtags that they are using. Ensure that you also use a few tags for your location such as "eyebrowtattoonewyork" and "newyork". This will enable you to be viewed when someone uses more specific search terms. Avoid using excessively long hashtags, it becomes hard to read and won't be a term that is searched for. Also avoid spamming posts with too many unrelated terms as it looks unprofessional. Always be careful with your spelling as you will miss out on reach and appear amateurish.

Once you have compiled your list of hashtags, keep them saved in the notes section of your phone for easy copy and pasting into Instagram. A common hack that many profiles use is to leave multiple lines of blank space between the post's caption and your hashtags. It looks neater and less spammy to use this method. If you have more than 30 hashtags then add them as a comment underneath your post. Research has shown that interactions are highest on IG posts which have more than 11 hashtags, so set this as the minimum to aim for.

Style Your Posts
A common trend amongst the most successful Instagram users is that they have a signature style for their photos. The posts often have a specific filter or pose used which makes the account stand out. Consistency is of prime

importance in brand recognition and awareness. You want potential clients to scroll through your feed and be familiar with your business, they should be able to guess who the post belongs to without reading the account name. When it comes to taking photos, aim for consistency with respect to editing, composition and angle. Play with the occasional bird's eye view or flat lay of your tattooing tools, use a quote on a background color that matches your logo, apply the same frame to your before/after shots, use natural lighting for the best contrast, keep your backdrops simple for a classy minimalist effect etc...

Be Responsive
Ensure that you are available to answer any private messages, questions or comments by your followers. This shows authenticity and professionalism, and builds happy customer relationships. Whether you are posting as an individual or under your brand name, it demonstrates that human side behind the

Instagram post. If you have a large following, this may consume a lot of your time. Nominate a particular half hour during your day to review notifications and respond to all queries at once, rather than one at a time. This ensures that you are less likely to miss a question and conditions followers not to expect instant replies. Hint: You can also tag yourself in a particular location, this increases familiarity for potential clients in the area.

Be Consistent

Similar to your Facebook business page, if you want to increase your Instagram following, you need to post on a regular basis to build your brand identity. Avoid making a surge of posts as this breaks that natural feel and gives a vibe of advertisement. Instagram users generally regard this type of behavior as spammy and will unfollow you.

To determine the best times to post, there are a number of tools (such as Squarelovin or

Iconosquare) which analyze when your community is most engaged and shows the best time to post for optimal exposure. Many of these tools provide decent insights just from using the free basic version. Use these insights to create a posting schedule and commit to it. It always helps to have a backlog posts or photos ready in advance so you can align to preferred timings.

Invite Engagement
Add an image or video with a call to action in the comments section. For example, you could upload a photo of your work with the request to "tag someone who would look great with these brows". Or put up a comical picture of someone with a monobrow and comment "Double tap if you think they need brow help" in the caption. Some cosmetic tattooists will ask their followers questions related to the post. Studies have shown that posts containing questions drive 300% more interaction than those without a call to action. Every post is an opportunity to increase engagement and build your customer

reach. Note that this should be a light hearted, non-salesy tactic and a fun thing for followers to respond to.

Contests and Promotions

For new Instagram users, this can be a great way to build engagement and increase your followers. A "like, comment, or tag your friends" contest is an easy way to do that. Simply post an image which offers a free treatment (perhaps one of your tattooing work) and tell people to like and comment why they deserve to win. You can also ask that they tag three other friends on Instagram to notify them of the contest. Choose a random winner from the entries, comment with the winner's handle, and follow through with delivery of the prize.

On the flipside, you could create a hashtag contest where users generate content to enter. This type of promotion is one of the newest and fun ways to engage your followers and expand your reach to wider networks. Below is an example of a caption you could use with your post:

> Today is the last day to enter my free eyebrow feathering competition. All you have to do is 1. Follow me 2. Share this post 3. Tag or mention my Instagram in your post as well as the hashtag #amyclarencompetition
> Good luck! Thanks to everyone who has entered so far, the winner will be drawn next week!

Be A Little Sneaky

Identify your key competitors and seek out their Instagram page. Under their "followers", you will find a listing of accounts which can include current clients, people who are interested in getting a cosmetic tattoo, and a proportion of spam-type or random accounts. Go through this list and add the genuine looking accounts one by one. This will need to be done gradually as Instagram limits the amount of adds you can make on an hourly basis. If you are ever waiting in line at the bank or for your meal then this is a great hack to pass time productively.

The beauty of this is that you are targeting a database of potential clients who are already interested in PMU and are likely to live in the area. Once you have added or requested to add private accounts, the user will get a notification and will review your Instagram. Expect to get a ten percent engagement rate using this method. That is, for every 100 people that you follow, about ten will follow you back. This can lead to eventual client bookings due to a greater reach. This is why you see some Instagram accounts who follow thousands of people, as it is a useful marketing tactic. After some time you can unfollow again as you have already made others aware of your business. Ensure that you have at least five quality photos of your work uploaded before you take this approach. People are unlikely to follow back an account that has no content.

Use the Location Feature

Is your business near a shopping mall or restaurant strip? Instagram allows you to view the photos of those who have uploaded a post and tagged the location (use the "Places" function). In this regard, they are likely to live nearby or in the area. You now have ready access to prospective clients, filtered by location. Search through the accounts of people who have posted in your area and target the gender/age of your ideal client. For example, use the Instagram search function to view all posts that have been tagged at the local Benny's Burgers. Then do a little more stalking and review the individual accounts of each post. If you find that most of your clients are females in their mid-twenties, then only follow the accounts which fit this demographic. As with the previous strategy, you will find that a proportion of individuals will follow back and thus keep your business in mind if they ever consider getting a cosmetic tattoo.

Seek Out Influencers

There is a whole industry of social media identities who have both brand appeal and a large following to boot. Some of these people are popular on Instagram only, whilst others leverage YouTube, blogs and other forums. Depending on the size of their following, some influencers will accept freebies in exchange for a post or review, whilst those who are more well known will charge for a post in addition to a complimentary product or treatment. Some boutique skin clinics and salons have experienced huge success just by offering free treatments to social media identities or celebrities. Followers who relate to these people are likely to trust their opinions and pay a premium to use the same services.

Seek out popular accounts on Instagram and see if their following fits your target clientele (preferably in your region). If they have contact details in their profile then this means they are usually open to endorsements or making sponsored posts which link to your account. Alternatively, you can private message them directly through Instagram. Reach out to the influencer and query if they are interested in a collaboration in exchange for a sponsored post. You may be surprised at the uptake as cosmetic tattooing is generally priced at the higher end of traditional freebies. Note that even smaller accounts with a following of 10,000 may be worth engaging with. Giving out one free treatment and having that exposure lead to another 10 bookings is worthwhile for a newbie cosmetic tattooist!

Track Your Metrics

Once you have a decent following and want to take it to the next level, consider using bit.ly to gauge the effectiveness of certain posts and campaigns. This popular URL link shortener is a useful tool which allows you to monitor how much traffic your Instagram account is driving to your site. If you were to just list your usual site address in your bio, it is impossible to track whether traffic is coming from Instagram as it is a mobile platform (Google analytics will show hits from online search results only).

Simply go to bitly.com and enter your full business website URL in the box at the top right of the screen. Click "Shorten" and you'll be taken to a page with your new shorter URL. Now just copy the link and paste into your IG account's bio. Then you can check your bit.ly data to document how many clicks your Instagram account is actually sending to your website. Use this knowledge to your advantage – work out which posts at certain times are optimal for converting into site traffic and replicate this.

Twitter

Twitter is a micro-blogging platform that allows people to follow individuals or businesses they are interested in to share information. This information is shared in short 140 character messages (called tweets) to their followers. Tweets appear on your follower's timeline feed on their computer or mobile phone when they are logged in to Twitter. If you tag a follower by name, they receive a notification letting them know they've been mentioned.

Twitter use by businesses is increasing fast. It is an effective platform to interact with consumers and generate repeat engagement rather than once-off messaging. Most Twitter users are under 50 years old and fit a younger, middle class, technically adept demographic. If your target cosmetic tattooing client base fits this profile then consider using this channel to promote your services, converse with potential clients, and to monitor trends in the PMU field by using hashtag searches. Using this platform will also help to build your online presence and supports your Google SEO ranking if you publish great content. Posts that obtain a lot of social shares are likely to get linked to by followers, which can influence your search engine results. If you choose to use Twitter to market your business, then follow the basic guidelines below:

Set Up Your Profile

Go online to register as a Twitter user and create a profile which contains a summary description of your business. Upload your logo image along with a link to your website (you can also use a bit.ly link here for tracking purposes). Your profile shows how many people follow you and who you are following, as well as the number of tweets you have generated.

Start Tweeting

Think about what content you would like to generate using your 140 character allowance. Note that all the tweets you create are visible on your Twitter profile and can be viewed by people searching for information about a particular topic (via hashtag usage), as well as by your followers. Your followers can reply to any tweet you send and they can also 'retweet' or on forward your tweet along to their followers. You can also send a direct message to other accounts by prefacing the message with DM. A tweet can include:

> **Hashtags -** A word beginning with the # sign. If a user clicks on these words then the search results for the term will be displayed. Conversely, someone searching for that term may see your tweet on the list of results. Use keywords from traditional SEO. This is a way your search and social teams can work synergistically together. Chances are Twitter users will also use some of the same keywords you've researched for your SEO campaign. Experiment with using them in tweets and as hashtags.

Mentions - The Twitter username of a business or individual. To send someone a mention, type his or her Twitter name anywhere within the tweet. If a user clicks on a mention it takes them to the mentioned business or person's Twitter profile.

Links to Web Content - Twitter automatically shortens links so they can fit in the character limit for a tweet. Leverage this to tweet out new blog posts or articles from your website.

Visual Content - Such as pictures of your work. If you don't want to duplicate marketing efforts, you can simply tweet out your Instagram posts.

Make Your Tweets Sharable

Get visual by engaging users with images and video content. These types of posts drive three to four more clicks on Twitter. Leverage your skills as a PMU artist and share your beauty tips (such as eyebrow shaping hacks, what style suits certain facial structures, how to pick a good cosmetic tattooist etc..). Ask questions to source the opinions of others using online survey programs such as Twtpoll. Run Twitter contests such as: "The next 10 people that retweet me will receive a treatment for 20 percent off". Being creative and fun in your posts all help to make your tweets more sharable, meaning more opportunities for you to get in front of your target market.

Interact With Others

Engage with your followers. Be sociable, follow others, retweet, and link to content of people you'd like to do the same for you. Try to do this with influencers in the cosmetic tattooing field. Interact with them on a regular basis to get your name out there. You can use the Twitter search function or tools such as like Followerwonk or Social Bearing to find like-minded prospects.

Be Strategic

Share useful content. Spread your tweets throughout the day and know when to post. There's lots of data out there about optimal times and quantities for tweeting.

Paid Advertising

Twitter offers a range of advertising services to help businesses promote themselves. Some options include promoted tweets to reach your target client demographic, and promotion of your account which can increase your follower base. Take a look at what other cosmetic tattooists are using the platform for and if their efforts appear to be successful. Replicate tried methods rather than using a non-conventional approach and wasting marketing spend. Failing to define exactly who you're trying to reach could cost you time and money. Remember, your ultimate aim is to develop relationships with potential clients and show your personality as a brand.

Reviews

In this interconnected society, customers have easy access to reviews and feedback about your business. Think about it, if you were about to be permanently tattooed on your face, wouldn't you do a bit (or a lot!) of research on your chosen artist? Clients are able to post their view of your work on forums such as Facebook, Yelp, Google, etc... They can even comment on your Instagram posts (although these can be deleted at your discretion). Throughout your career as a cosmetic tattooist, it is inevitable that you will generate some great responses and some more negative ones. Unfortunately, the negative ones can be quite demotivating and dig away at your confidence. To minimize these, ensure that you are consistent with your customer service and provide clients with that extra care factor. This all ties in with your brand's reputation. Even if someone is quite unhappy with the result, offer to fix it or refund their fee. Being professional and empathetic about the situation can avoid an anger fuelled review post later on. This can deter prospective customers and undermine your credibility. If you do get those poor review posts anyway, respond to them in a compassionate and fair manner.

On the flipside, reviews can generate great business if viewed as genuine. Similar to word of mouth referrals, one happy customer boast can lead to multiple bookings over time. Actively solicit this type of feedback from your happy clients. Ask them to leave you an honest review on your Facebook page or Google search engine result. Be tactful with the people whom you ask to do this – ensure they are the satisfied ones! You can also leave a short message on your aftercare forms which are provided to clients post-treatment. A sample request could be worded as below:

Thank you for trusting us with your cosmetic tattoo! We aim to provide you with a great natural enhancement and service! As always, the highest complement you can give us is a referral ♥

- *Facebook business page link*
- *Yelp business page link*

Leverage Yourself

As a PMU artist, your key source of income will be from initial treatments and touch-ups. It is likely that the type of person who would get a cosmetic tattoo would be quite beauty-conscious and be open to other treatments. Leveraging upon secondary income sources can help to pay those business overheads and allow you to get ahead without too much more effort. Some options include:

- Providing additional treatments such as eyelash extensions or lash perms. These can be included as a package deal with the tattoo or on their own to fill vacant appointment slots.

- Selling quality items which relate to tattoo maintenance. This can include after-care oils, emollient creams, sunscreens, and even make up items which further define the tattoo.

- Offering gift vouchers for specific services. You can tie these offers to promotional periods such as Thanksgiving or Labor Day. People generally have more time off to heal from a treatment during these holidays so make the most of this.

- Becoming a PMU trainer (subject to the requirements of your locale). Once you have the depth of experience and capability, consider taking on an apprentice or teaching fellow artists your technique. Many well-known cosmetic tattooists end up doing this as there is high demand for quality training. Note that there are some poor quality courses out there where artists are operating unethically. That is, they are underqualified to teach others and risk damaging the reputation of the PMU industry. Do not consider training if you are not 100% confident in your ability and have the results to back it up.

Mistakes to avoid

A career in the cosmetic tattooing industry can often mean late nights and no weekends. In this regard, you want to ensure that your time is spent productively, focusing on tasks that truly add value. Be wary of the following common marketing mistakes and incorporate them into your strategy:

Not Identifying Your Target Market

Sounds simple right? Basically anyone who wants a cosmetic tattoo. Having such a broad reach means that your efforts to source clients will not command that "must-have" appeal that you need. Define your key group. Look at their average salary and adjust your pricing to suit. Study their social media use habits and preferred online forums. Cater your language and posts to this market. It is always better to capture 20% of clients in a particular subset rather than 0% of the whole market.

Getting Your Pricing Wrong

This is linked to your target market research. Some cosmetic tattooists grossly undervalue themselves and end up sending the wrong message about the quality of their brand. Finding the right price point is one of the hardest tasks you face in your new venture. Set your prices too high, and potential new customers will be put off. Set them too low, and you may be taking on additional clients just to cover the bills. If clients are re-booking and new customers don't sound surprised when you quote a price, then you're probably on the ball.

Not Replicating Success

There are a number of high-profile cosmetic tattooists around the world who have enviable waiting lists. How did they get there? Keep tabs on what they are (and aren't) doing. Even if they do not operate in your area, review other businesses like yours that are doing well and study their marketing. Pay attention to what tactics they use on a regular basis and learn from their mistakes. You don't want to be the one gambling on an innovative campaign, you want to model those who have tried and tested methods. Expend your energy and marketing budget on proven tactics rather than guesswork.

Not Standing Out From The Masses

As a first step, you should always review who your key competitors are and what their unique selling proposition (USP) is. Do they specialize in cosmetic tattooing only or is it part of a full salon menu? Are their services much more comprehensive than yours? If so, how can you position your offering to stand out? Frame your USP so that you are differentiated from the masses. Incorporate your approach into all aspects of the business (e.g. using high quality products, having a very classy website, providing better service to clients such as follow up calls). You need to have the same look and feel across all of your ads, promotions, and overall marketing materials. Even simple things such as having articles about permanent make-up (which you have written as an "expert" in the field) on your website can make a great impression.

Sloppy Content

It is sometimes mind-boggling how often spelling errors and mistakes make it into marketing content. From wrongly spelt hashtags to poorly worded captions, these can easily damage the reputation of your brand. Your business will come off as unprofessional and sloppy. If you need some help on the grammar front then engage with a language savvy friend to do a quick review or hire a freelance copywriter.

Being A Perfectionist

In this industry, it is often the first in best dressed. Cosmetic tattooing is becoming somewhat viral due to the "feathering" craze and those on the market already are reaping the rewards. Although you should focus on making your brand and marketing tools high quality, do not spend all your time in revising content and design over and over. Build up your client base and add better quality portfolio shots. Investing in perfection too early may yield few results. You can always keep your branding simple initially and work on this over time. New business owners tend to use the set-up phase as procrastination from doing work that produces financial results!

Not Tracking Results

How do you know what works if you don't track your efforts. Does posting on Instagram result in an influx of bookings? Does a Facebook post result in many click-through's to your website? There are a number of tools such as Google Analytics where you can view conversions from advertising investments. Ensure that you track your return on investment or risk failure to improve or refine.

Not Budgeting For Marketing

After paying for quality equipment and décor expenses of a new set-up, your budget can easily be inflated. Do not get too carried away with overspending. There are many ways to be thrifty and still appear professional and high-end. Your business still needs to look the part, but if you have no cash left over to promote it then no clients will come!

Conclusion

There are many ways in which you can build your brand online and via your networks. Each PMU artist will be more inclined to use some methods than others. Pick a few which best suit your business and be consistent with your marketing. After some time, you may find that word of mouth and simply the viral nature of the internet will drive bookings without much effort. This is not uncommon within the cosmetic tattooing field, and some practitioners find themselves inundated with requests. Work hard and ethically, keep developing your artistic ability, and you may very well find yourself in this position!

One Last Thing...

If you enjoyed this book or found it useful I'd be very grateful if you'd post a short review on Amazon.

Your support really does make a difference and I read all the reviews personally so I can get your feedback and make this book even better.

Thanks again for reading!

Leila xx

Made in the USA
Middletown, DE
31 May 2019